Once upon a Pancake

FOR YOUNGER STORYTELLERS

Stories We
Write Together

PFANNKUCHEN PRESS

WRITTEN BY

THAT'S YOU! ↗
WRITE YOUR NAMES

STARTED BY **Rick Benger**

LEAD ILLUSTRATION BY **Maddie Egremont**

EDITED BY **Karin Fisher-Golton**

COVER DESIGN BY **Kristen Haff**

A NOTE FOR GROWN-UPS

This book is suitable for children of ages 6–8 (or so), who are typically learning to read and write. You'll help by doing the bulk of the reading and writing, to keep the stories going and the creativity flowing. It's best to transcribe word-for-word, so the children can fully experience the power of their own storytelling. Don't worry about tying the stories up with beginnings, middles, and ends—the joy is in setting the imagination free and capturing creativity on the page.

The real magic begins when you take turns to imagine what happens next. It helps to use different colors for each storyteller, e.g. red for Maria, green for Harry, blue for Mom.

HAVE FUN!
RICK

P.S. For finished story examples and other creative inspiration, take a peek at our Instagram (@uponapancake) and website (onceuponapancake.com).

H azel was reading a wonderful book called ....
....

    She was very tired but wanted to keep reading. She kept her eyes open as long as she could, which wasn't long. She fell asleep and started to dream about

....

....

....

....

....

....

....

....

....

....

....

....

DRAW HAZEL'S
DREAM

WHAT HAPPENED
WHEN HAZEL
WOKE UP?

STORY #1

O f all the superpowers, I got a silly one—the ability to

....

....

But a silly superpower isn't going to stop me from being awesome. And that means I need an awesome costume.

DRAW THE
COSTUME!

I finish creating my costume and put it on. Perfect. Time to really try out my new superpower.

HOW?
WHERE?

KEEP GOING . . .

STORY #2

... CONTINUED

IS ANYBODY ELSE
INVOLVED? GOOD
GUYS? BAD GUYS?

Nathan is hungry. He opens the fridge and *SPLAT*, something greasy hits him in the face.

"Get down!" says a squeaky little voice.

"What . . . who said that!?" says Nathan.

"Me!"

Nathan sees that a tiny elf is speaking. The elf is hiding behind the butter dish, making little butter-balls.

It's the final soccer game of the season, and Sara is full of worry.

Usually, Jayden plays goalkeeper. But Jayden is sick, and the coach picked Sara to take his place.

The other team kicks off the first half. Then

WHAT DOES SARA DO?

STORY #4

Olivia has exactly seventeen minutes and twenty-one seconds to save the galaxy. Yikes.

First, she has to figure out what happened. She looks around the spaceship control deck for clues.

WHAT DOES SHE NOTICE?

WHERE DID THE CAPTAIN GO?

KEEP GOING . . .

00:17:21
until it all
goes boom!

STORY #5

...CONTINUED

6 MINUTES AND
42 SECONDS
LEFT!

UH-OH. ONLY 30
SECONDS TO GO!

Lucas the little puff of wind doesn't want to leave his cloud and start the day.

"I'm too tired to get up!" he tells his parents.

"But what about the sailboats?" they ask. "Without you, how will they move across the bay?"

"I'm just a little puff. I can't move them much."

"What about the fuzzy balls on the dandelions? How will they float away and find new places to grow?"

"I'm just a tiny breeze," says Lucas. "I won't help them much."

"What about

DOES LUCAS
GET UP FROM
HIS CLOUD?

My friends and I are playing Hide and Seek. I'm It.

I finish counting and call out, "Ready or not, here I come!"

It's easy to find Tony the Turtle. He is near the ....

....

Next I find ....

....

....

....

....

....

....

....

....

....

....

KEEP GOING . . .

FIVE FRIENDS TO FIND! LOOK FOR A TURTLE, →
A TOUCAN, A JAGUAR, A MONKEY, AND A CHAMELEON.
(HINT: THE CHAMELEON LOOKS LIKE THIS 🦎.)

STORY #7

STORY #7

...CONTINUED

FOUND THEM ALL?
NOW WHAT HAPPENS?

STORY #7

Fatima's favorite store is called Quirk & Quirk's Old Stuff and Thingamabobs. Everything inside is old, rare, or downright weird.

One afternoon, Fatima walks by Quirk & Quirk's and sees something new in the window—a can of rainbow paint. Cool! She walks in and buys the can.

WHAT DOES
FATIMA PAINT?

WHAT HAPPENS
WHEN SHE FINISHES
PAINTING?

"I told you not to go to the top of Muddle Mountain," says Grandma Lion. "Remember? I said you'd get . . . "

"Mixed up!" says Baby Giraffe.

"Messed up!" says Baby Elephant.

"Muddled up!" says Baby Ostrich.

"Exactly," says Grandma Lion. "But I can see you went up there anyway. Just look at you! Your tops and bottoms are all switched around!"

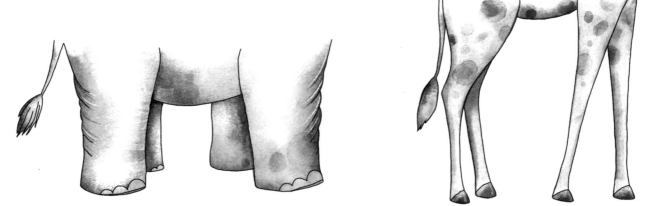

KEEP GOING . . .

DRAW THE BABY
ANIMALS!

DO THE
BABY ANIMALS
GET UNMUDDLED?

M

arco wakes up to perfect Saturday weather—rain. Rain means his parents won't make him go outside and play. He can stay inside all day and invent things.

He reaches under his bed, pulls out his box of treasures, and dumps everything on the floor.

WHICH TREASURES DOES MARCO USE?

WHAT DOES
MARCO DO WITH
HIS INVENTION?

I was playing basketball with .... WHO? when I heard a deep rumble and a loud buzz. I looked around. There was a spaceship landing at the other end of the court.

Its door went *whoosh* and out came some aliens, cool and casual, as though it was no big deal.

They didn't look like you'd expect.

....

....

....

DESCRIBE
THE ALIENS

....

....

....

Then one of them said, " ....

....

....

....

....

....

....

STORY #11

In Maya's house, there was a big old grandfather clock.

TICK, its pendulum swung to the left.

TOCK, its pendulum swung to the right.

TICK, TOCK went the old grandfather clock—until it stopped.

It stopped between a *TICK* and a *TOCK,* and the whole world stopped too.

Maya's dad froze mid-sneeze, between the *AH* and the *CHOO.*

Maya's dog froze mid-bark, between the *BOW* and the *WOW.*

But Maya didn't freeze. Time had stopped but not for her.

WHAT HAPPENED
WHEN TIME
STOPPED?

KEEP GOING . . .

... CONTINUED

DID TIME START
AGAIN? HOW?

Mike was getting bored of Halloween, mainly because his mom always made him go trick-or-treating with his little sister.

But free candy was free candy. So Mike went along, dressed up as

His sister dressed up as

It was a successful night. Mike's bag was full, and he was happy. He and his sister decided to walk home.

On the way, Mike stopped, surprised, at the gate of a small house. He had never noticed the house before, even though he must have walked along this street a hundred times. There was a pumpkin on the porch, but no lights were on.

Mike's sister stopped too.

"Let's go home," Mike said. "We've got enough anyhow."

"You scared?" his sister teased.

SOUNDS CREEPY! WHAT DID THEY DO?

STORY #13

A boy was sitting on the edge of a pier, watching a fish swim below.

"I wish I was that fish," thought the boy. "Then I would swim down deep, and

That same fish was watching a seagull fly by.

"I wish I was that seagull," thought the fish. "Then I would fly high above the sea, and

And the seagull was watching the boy on the pier.

"I wish I was that boy," thought the seagull. "Then I would

WHAT HAPPENED NEXT?

STORY #15

STORY #15

Grandpa is giving Imani an amazing birthday gift—an extra special party. Any kind of party she wants.

There's just one problem. Imani has two great ideas, and she can't decide which one to choose!

"Why don't you make a list?" says Grandpa. "Compare your ideas side by side."

Imani smiles and grabs a pad and pencil.

FILL IN THE LIST!

IDEA: _____

IDEA: _____

WHAT DOES
IMANI DECIDE?

HOW DOES THE
PARTY GO?

Gogorath the demon pirate is having an unlucky day—one of those days when a teeny thing makes a bigger thing happen, which makes an even bigger thing happen, and before you know it there's a mighty ruckus.

The teeny thing at the start of Gogorath's day was that he knocked his jellyfish juice off the breakfast table. Then

And then

And then

WHAT WAS THE
MIGHTY RUCKUS?

A lex lives in a mushroom.

It took Addison and her friends eight hours, five hot chocolate breaks, and three changes of dry gloves and socks, but it was finally done — the biggest snowman ever.

Happy and tired, they all went inside for dinner. Midway through her second bowl of spaghetti, Addison heard a *thump thump thump* outside.

She opened the back door to see what was going on. The snowman was gone.

Meanwhile, the snowman was

KEEP GOING . . .

STORY #19

Thisis ...., goddess of the Sun and ....

Now there are three things you need to know about
....

First, you'd never guess, but she is one thousand years old. Second, she ....

....

.... And third,

she ....

....

....

One afternoon she was lying in the park, listening

to ....

...., when

....

....

STORY #20

STORY #20

MORE STORIES?

AT **ONCEUPONAPANCAKE.COM** YOU'LL FIND:

the full children's series

free teachers' guides and story packs

the coffee table book (for grown-ups)

Published in Menlo Park, California in 2020 by Pfannkuchen Press LLC.

Copyright © 2019 by Rick Benger. All rights reserved.

Original illustrations by Maddie Egremont in stories 2, 5, 10, and 14; by Matej Beg in story 4; and by Daniel Howard in story 7. These and the original illustrations in stories 3, 8, 15, and 19 are owned by Pfannkuchen Press. All other images and adapted images are licensed via Shutterstock.

Library of Congress Control Number: 2020933987

ISBN: 978-0-9993961-2-4

First edition. Printed and bound in Canada.